Digging Deeper

Maggie Bamburg

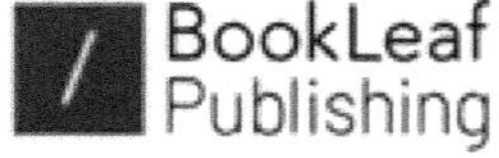

Presentation by *BookLeaf Publishing*

Web: www.bookleafpub.com

E-mail: info@bookleafpub.com

ISBN : 9789357210775

First edition 2022

PREFACE

Life can be overwhelming.
Take time to enjoy the little things;
Question the big things.
Appreciate those that love you for who you are,
Including yourself.

When it Rains...

In the early morning the sky wept.
Her tears made puddles along the sidewalk,
they rushed down streets, they clung to my
window and in my hair.
She left me cold and yet I danced in the open,
urging her to look down.
I wanted her to know that from her tears flowers
would grow.
The grass would grow greener and taller.
That people will not take shelter, but rather grab
hands and run through every drop.
That we would take umbrellas and buckets and
gather her sadness.
I wanted her to know that when her tears washed
over the earth we rejoiced, we felt reborn.
I wanted her to know we were not afraid and
that we've all felt like
our tears might drown the ones we love.

... it Pours

He smelled like the rain.
The dew lingering in the threads of his sweater.
He smelled like mud puddle fights and running
through the sprinkler in May.
I used to hate the rain,
but now when it starts to pour, I think of the
purest of love,
and the feeling of soft kisses against my skin.

Cicada Song

I felt at peace there, surrounded by emerald
green,
Listening to the cicadas chirp, following my
footsteps.
How can something so small make so much
sound?
You, cicada remind me what humans should be:
Piercing, playful, perplexing.
You, cicada are not just a bug.
You house a beautiful voice.
You remind me we are not just bodies,
but beauty in disguise.

Wishing Well

My hands plunge beneath the surface.
The cold slipping between each finger.
I want to fall in, I want to be weightless.
I want to sink to the bottom of the sea and feel
the concrete scrape my knees.
I want to live here, sink here, never escape.
I want the water to consume me, swallow me,
and never spit me out.

As above...

I lay in the grass feeling the soil sink below me.
I convince myself I can feel the earth spin below
me.
The golden rays of the sun lay gently across my
face.
I squint into the seamless blue.
I feel as if I could float off leaving the whole
universe behind.
My atoms and your atoms
combined
until the end of time.

...So below

My back against the bed of your truck.
My heart racing, pounding, leaping.
I look towards the sky.
Black. Pitch, dark, black.
Nothing more.
The empty sky dragging me in.
I reach.
My fingertips searching for another universe
beyond me.
I melt into the nothingness.
I am the sky.
We are one.

Ashes to Ashes

Grandmother sits on her green velvet couch. Legs crossed, lips pursed, she leans in for a kiss. Her wine-colored lipstick against my cheek. I glance at her old and fragile hands that sit upon her lap. Her nails shine with a glossy finish. They were always perfect. She clasps her Marlboro between her boney fingers like its the only thing keeping her alive. Tapping the small bit of cigarette she has left, she shakes loose the ashes, her lipstick staining the edges. My mother always hated that smell, but to me it was not the smell of tobacco. It smelled like the old sweaters that hung in her closet. It smelled like childhood memories. It smelled sweet. A smell I couldn't resist. With each puff I inhale her scent.

Soul or Sole?

Sometimes I wonder... if I put on a different pair of shoes in the morning would my path change? Is my future woven into these old laces? If I pick my worn out boots, will gardens would swarm the soles of my feet? Will rains take over and vines encapsulate my tongue, making it impossible to walk? Stuck in vegetation, I would ask myself: Why couldn't you have just picked a different pair? As if something that simple could save me.

Eublepharis Macularius

As morbid as it sounds I always liked the way I
looked when I was done crying.
My eyes the perfect mix of green and gold. Like
they had decided to take a walk through luscious
forests. My face showed its true tone: red and
speckled. Like a gecko with its head tilted
toward the sun. My head lifted high, as if I never
let anything consume me in the first place.

A Collector of Sorts

Who am I? I am the person who puts olives on the end of my fingers before I eat them. I am the person who names inanimate objects because I feel some sort of connection with them. I am the person who stops in the middle of five o'clock traffic and picks turtles up off the road. I am the person who can't decide if the glass is half full or half empty, but rather just something to drink out of. I am the person who still doesn't know how to ride a bike after 18 years of living. I am the person who collects life's little moments. I am the person who thinks the mundane is the reason for living. I am the soul that houses inside me. I am nothing more than you want me to be.

The (For)giving Tree

We were both in bad places
so we made a good place together.
Where we both lay in silence
staring at the rustling trees.
Forgiving the other
for we are not forgiving ourselves.

Too Many Questions

I asked why for a long time.
But the truth was I didn't need to wonder,
Because somehow I knew all along;
Even mistakes can be beautiful.

Skipping Stones

I toss a pebble,
let it bounce across the lake;
my heart skips with it.

Hive Mind

I remember it. I remember being in and out of doctors offices since I was 11. I remember not being able to breathe and having oxygen tubes threaded below my nose. I remember those Jellyfish-like wires attached to my scalp. I felt as if it knew my every thought. I felt like it was infiltrating my brain, making me weaker. I sat there drowning beneath its tentacles. A part of me hoped that hive-minded jellyfish would be able to read my brain. I wanted it to know everything. I wanted answers. I wanted to know why it was necessary to have wires hanging from head to toe. I wanted to know why I felt heavy and why I slept so much. Tell me all knowing Jelly, can you save me?

Till death...

I never was the religious type. Not that I didn't try to be. I went to church. I bowed my head while others hummed their prayer, and when my eyes returned to the pulpit two boys came out with crackers and wine. I spent the rest of the night crying in the basement of that church. The irony being that I still cared what God thought even though I didn't believe in him. And when I cried, I was told it was because I had a connection with God. That feeling guilty meant I was going to be saved. The irony being that I didn't want to be saved. I wanted to be at peace. At peace with the thought of dying. At peace knowing there will be someone welcoming me after death.

...Do us part

It seemed so wonderful to be absent from the fear of death, because you knew where you were going. You knew his hands were going to pull you from the earth and say welcome to heaven. I would say this... this is not heaven. Living forever is not heaven. Feeling guilty is not heaven. Heaven is simply being where you are. Heaven is when you come home with the smell of Merlot on your lips, when you reach in for a kiss. It's when you open a chapter of your favorite book. It's when you kiss the dogs goodnight because you once told me "all dogs go to heaven." It's when you tell me heaven is real, maybe just not in the traditional sense. You tell me to keep an open mind. Because one day our bones will lay side by side beneath six feet of earth. And maybe, just maybe, God will be there to pluck us from the dirt. I never was the religious type, but when you spoke about God, I felt as if I could sit in a heaven that did not exist.

Death's Scythe

Death is not a looming monster who preys on those in their weakest moments and plucks them from the earth. Death is not a hooded figure of grim and despair. For under deaths cloak grows a bed of flowers. His pockets filled with purpose. Deaths scythe cuts weeds beneath our feet, allowing a peaceful path to the underworld. He carries our fragile flesh in his rusty bones. Death assures company on our journey. Death is a keeper of souls. Our souls, however, are not trapped behind bars. No, our souls, our bodies, our minds, are recycled. Because of death, we are allowed to rest in a new life, a new world.

Green Thumb

I wanted to grow, so I bought a few plants at the
local market.
I tried so hard to make those flowers bud.
I sat there day after day hoping for a sprout.
I tried to take care of them, but I either watered
too much or too little.
I realized in that moment I did the same to
myself.
I wanted myself to grow,
So I over watered,
Then gave up entirely.
I caused a drought,
Yet expected myself to bloom.

Ignorance is Bliss

There was a saying I once heard,
it read:
"The day you plant the seed is not the day you
eat the fruit."
I remember thinking it was silly
Because I stuffed my face with berries as a child,
not worried about where they grew from or how.
All I cared about was the pleasant taste they left
behind.
As a child I did not care for those seeds.
I would spit them out every chance I got and
leave the stem.
I would let the juice drip down my fingers
then wipe them on my pants, without a care in
the world,
Staining my once blue jeans.
No amount of scrubbing could ever get rid of it.

Bitter Sweet

This morning I ordered your favorite coffee.
I never liked the taste,
it was always too bitter.
But I was missing you, missing the way we used
to be.
So I took a sip, then another.
It always burnt my tongue; I was never patient
enough.
After that first sip, our memories flooded my
brain.
I hated this coffee, but I love you.
So I take a sip.
I would pick you over my favorite coffee any
day.

The Waltz of Life

Our feet in synch, swiftly sliding across the
wooden floor.
The smell of maple syrup filling the air.
I hear our socks sliding as you spin me around
the kitchen.
My feet stumble stepping on your toes.
You kiss my forehead, your warm breath against
my skin.
The room smells of burnt waffles.
Our breakfast forgotten.

Decades later, our bodies now frail our minds
growing old.
My hand lays in yours, our feet still dancing.
We waddle to Frank Sinatra, our food growing
cold.
Forever in my heart you'll be dancing.

One day we'll reach heaven...
And together we will be doing the Waltz for
eternity.